Hafiz

Hafiz

An Offering

Translated by

FARRUKH DHONDY

in association with

FIRDOUS ALI

HARPERPERENNIAL

An Imprint of HarperCollins *Publishers*

First published in English in India by Harper Perennial 2023
An imprint of HarperCollins *Publishers*
4th Floor, Tower A, Building No. 10, DLF Cyber City,
DLF Phase II, Gurugram, Haryana – 122002
www.harpercollins.co.in

2 4 6 8 10 9 7 5 3 1

P-ISBN: 978-93-5699-609-0
E-ISBN: 978-93-5699-610-6

Typeset in 11/15.5 Bell MT Std at
Manipal Technologies Limited, Manipal

Printed and bound at
Thomson Press (India) Ltd

MIX
Paper from responsible sources
FSC® C010615

This book is produced from independently certified FSC® paper to ensure responsible forest management.

To the memory of Firdous Ali

Hafiz, An Introduction

THE fourteenth-century (1325-1390) Persian poet Hafiz is probably the most favoured poet of that language in Persia, though not as internationally renowned as his predecessor Jalaluddin Rumi.

Hafiz was born in Shiraz, in south-east Persia, in 1325. He was named Shams-ud-din Muhammed. His father, a coal merchant with a failing trade, died when Shams was young, leaving his mother and two older brothers behind. The brothers left Shiraz to seek employment in other cities, and Shams and his mother went to live with his uncle.

At an early age, Shams was put to work, first as a porter in a drapery and then in a bakery, where the proprietor would, each mealtime, mostly evenings, bake fresh naans from the clay ovens for queues of local clientele who'd take them home for dinner. Shams would have assisted, kneading the dough, rolling it out, baking it in the ovens or extracting them from the heat with long tongs.

The young Shams, under the tutelage of his father and perhaps of mullahs, was said to have memorized the entire Quran and could recite it at an early age. Scholars who achieved this were given the title of

Hafiz, and this is what he called himself when he began to write and publish verse.

There are very few testaments to his life, but it is more than probable that, at an early age, he was exposed to the Persian poets popular at that time in Shiraz, the principal one being Saadi, the city's iconic voice of the time. Some accounts or myths of his life and accomplishments maintain that, apart from the Quran, he had memorized and could recite the whole oeuvre of the poets Rumi, Saadi and Nizami. If it were true, it would make him the human supercomputer of his time as the Masnavi of Rumi alone contains 25,000 couplets or 50,000 lines.

A legendary account of his life recounts that at the age of twenty-one, besides having memorized the Quran and the entire works of several poets, he had mastered the Turkish and Arabic languages. He was still earning his living at the bakery. One day, required to deliver naans to the more prosperous houses who wouldn't deign to join the queues in the street, he caught a glimpse of a young woman on a balcony. She was from a rich, upper-class family and her name was Shakh-e-nabat, which means 'branch of sugarcane'. Shams was instantly and helplessly infatuated. The story says he fainted on the spot (but fails to tell us what happened to the delivery of those naans).

His fascination led him to carry out a ritual penance of staying awake for forty nights by the shrine of Baba Kuhi, a saint of Shiraz. Again, the story says nothing about having a nap during the day. The penance, the legend surrounding the shrine claimed, would be rewarded with the gift of poesy, of immortality or by being granted the penitent's heart's desire.

Shams began the ritual hoping for the latter. As he stayed by the shrine through those nights, the angel Gabriel appeared to him and, by the effulgent beauty of his presence, converted Shams's heart's desire – from the pursuit of a woman to the pursuit of God.

The angel Gabriel directed Shams to the house, and thence the feet, of a Sufi master called Mohammed Attar, who was to pass on the doctrines of Sufism to him over the years.

He was thus granted the gift of poetry, which, surviving all these centuries in the original and in translation, must mean he gained immortality of a literary sort at least. So the penance had brought him all three promised rewards.

Shams took on the 'takallus', the pen name, of Hafiz and began to write paeans to his beloved Shakh-e-nabat. These verses, it is said, came to her attention and she reciprocated the poet's love, though she was promised in marriage to a prince of Persia and he was already married.

The constant theme of separation in his verse, though traditional in Sufi poetry to express a longing for unity with God and a lament for being apart from the Almighty, can be read in Hafiz as a complaint against the barriers to his love for this 'beloved'.

Hafiz gained great renown through his verses and was patronized by the rulers of Shiraz. The longest reigning of these was Shah Shuja, who befriended Hafiz and was something of a poet himself. Very many of Hafiz's compositions were attacks on the hypocrisy of organized religion and on the mullahs, who propagated it with juridical vigour.

Through Rumi and the poetical traditions of Persia, Hafiz had adopted the Sufi interpretation of Islam, and indeed of life and being. His expressions of the Sufi faith, which rejects juridical Islam, gained him the enmity of the Islamic theologians in Shiraz and in the courts. They began a campaign against him and what they considered his heretical verses.

Hafiz's verses ridiculing poets he considered inferior to himself may have offended the king of Shiraz, Shah Shuja, who considered himself a poet.

Whether it was the political manoeuvring of these clerical critics or whether the ridicule he poured on poets lesser than himself, which Shah Shuja took to heart, that caused Hafiz to hastily flee from Shiraz is not certain. One or the other, or both, caused Hafiz to take his wife and belongings, and suddenly leave the city to go to Isfahan and then to Yazd.

The fact that he had a wife to whose beauty or devotion he wrote not one verse is probably not puzzling or paradoxical. Marriage at the time was not a matter of mutual attraction and love, but an arrangement whereby families created bonds. Hafiz is reputed to have maintained, through these years, his devotion to the sugar-cane lady to whom his expressions of love and longing are directed.

In one of his verses, Hafiz respectfully mentions taking refuge in the 'fire-temple'. There were no fire-temples in Shiraz where he had spent his life before his flight to Yazd. Would this be a reference to the place of worship of Zoroastrian Iranians who still existed in Yazd in his time? Scholars have traced the philosophical roots of Sufism to pre-Islamic Zoroastrianism. Was Hafiz, in this single verse, acknowledging such a connection? And would that verse be counted as a heresy by Islamic clerics?

In his exile from Shiraz, Hafiz is reputed to have come across the Central Asian 'Turkish' conqueror Timur-i-lang, or Tamerlane to Christopher Marlowe and Europeans. The story goes that he was summoned by Timur, who had by then raided India and occupied parts of Persia. Timur was disturbed by a verse of Hafiz's which said he would exchange the cities of Samarkand and the beautified Bokhara for the black mole on his beloved's body. This is purported to have angered Timur whose capital was Samarkand and whose most illustrious city was Bokhara. When Hafiz appeared before him as a supplicant, Timur demanded why he had impudently said that his principal cities were worth less than a mole on some Shirazi woman's body. Hafiz humbly replied that this was the sort of foolish thought that had brought him to the condition of poverty, which the conqueror could see before him.

Timur, impressed by the wit of the rejoinder, sent Hafiz away with elaborate gifts.

Shah Shuja, motivated by regret at Hafiz's absence, or through wanting to defy the orthodox Islamic clerics of Shiraz with whom he had developed violent religious disagreements, invited Hafiz to return to Shiraz. The scorn Hafiz had poured on inferior poets, was apparently forgotten or forgiven.

On his return to Shiraz at Shah Shuja's invitation and his reinstatement as a teacher and court poet, he resumed his role of 'murid' or disciple of the Sufi master.

In the fortieth year of his pupillage to Attar, Hafiz undertook a ritual trial through which he isolated himself in a circle that he drew in the ground and remained within it for forty days. This penance of self-imprisonment completed, he hurried to his master's house and Attar blessed him, gave him a glass of wine and declared that he had attained the enlightenment that meant a Union with The Beloved.

In Sufi lore, this transcendence is called Realization and it endowed Hafiz with the gift, or perhaps the confidence, to write theosophical verse and teach, through verse, the precepts of Sufism.

Through the last year of his life, Hafiz suffered from a disease that caused him extreme pain. In 1390, he died with the conviction that death was part of the continuity of existence.

The clerical officials of Shiraz denied this scion of the people a Muslim burial.

His supporters and those who had absorbed the message of his verses argued that the mullah's permission or blessing was not a ticket to the afterlife, but that Hafiz's faith itself ensured that he was on the path to paradise.

Neither in this brief introduction to a book of translated verse, nor in the blogs or volumes of those who profess to be Sufi savants, can one conclusively define what Sufism is or means.

It purports to be the true interpretation of Islam, breaking with juridical, clerical and, in today's world, terrorist and death-cult versions of the religion.

Sufis quote two main Suras of the Quran, the Word of God, as foundations of their belief. God, the ultimate, is not then an anthropomorphic presence, in some unseen space or universe, but the spirit of life and energy in the heart of all mortals. The goal of the Sufi quest is unity with this energy, the merging of the separated drop of water, the metaphor for the individual soul, with the vast ocean of the Beloved from whence the drop came.

The poetry of Sufis, inseparable from the expression of belief, is the theology of this religion of Islam.

The Masnavi, the six-volume work of Jalaludin Rumi, Hafiz's predecessor and inspiration, is known as the Quran in verse.

Its tenets, which the poetry of Hafiz (religiously?) follows is that the spiritual quest of life is the unity with the divine.

The divine then is represented in Sufi writings as The Beloved, as The Friend, as Him, as You – and then as the lover, the one with hypnotic eyes, with enslaving tresses of hair, with a mole on the features of the loved one that captures and enslaves. And then again as the Sun, the Moon, the Rose garden or even the voice of the nightingale.

Most persistently, Sufi theology embraces the idea that pure logic, pure ratiocination, rationality are chains and constraints on the soul. They are manifestations of the ego, the separateness of the individual from the ocean of energy, the barrier of illusion, which prevents or inhibits the merging of the seeker with The Beloved. The path to the merger is consequently an abandonment of reason and an embrace of a state of denial of reason's constraints.

The metaphor for this state of being in Sufi literature is intoxication. Thus, the means to the merger with God becomes the abandonment of the ego and the symbolic agents of transition to such a state are the Saki, the tavern-keeper and the goblet of wine. In the tradition that derives from Rumi, the followers of Sufi dance in a symbolic show of abandonment and intoxication.

The Sufi poetic tradition, professing love for the almighty, The Beloved, employed the images of earthly romantic fascination, union, separation, longing of man for woman as metaphors. These states of infatuation or inebriation stand for devotion to, longing for, love of and the desperation of separation from the presence of or unity with God.

In the works of Rumi, this metaphor appears to remain pure. When he appeals in his poetry to a lover, he means the Almighty or indeed the person whom Rumi thought of as the manifestation of His wisdom on earth, his spiritual guide, Shams-u-Tabrez.

In the works of Hafiz, a century later, the metaphor's intention very subtly or even blithely turns literal. The

Beloved is often the beloved. In his poems, there is an ambivalence of the metaphor. The distinction between love for the divine and earthly love for a woman is not quite as distinct as in Rumi. In other words, when he talks of love and The Beloved, he could mean God and it could be interpreted as the woman to whom he is devoted or an object of human longing.

The Beloved, true to the traditions of Sufi poetry, is clearly a divine presence. Translating Hafiz's meaning as earthly romance may pander to the contemporary reader's passion for the girl next door (or glimpsed on the balcony?), but it corrupts Hafiz's religious intention. The Sufi tradition allows that every act of human affection is a tribute to the divine.

As an embattled, if historically triumphant, interpretation of Islam, Sufis in their poetry attacked what they considered plebeian and mistakenly ritualistic, pedantic and punitive versions of Islam. They expressed these strictures in their poetic attacks on the opposing clerics and have won, even to this day, the excommunicating venom of fundamentalist cults such as the Saudi Arabian-led Wahhabis.

Hafiz inherits and uses the conventional imagery of Persian poetry: The rose, the garden, the nightingale, musk, aloe, the tall cypress of aloofness and majesty, the gaze, the eyes, the eyebrows of the beloved … And then the supposed sexuality of the beloved's tresses. Does the tradition of the compulsory covering of female hair in the traditions of some denominations of Islam come from the conviction that female hair is an object of sexual attraction? The tresses in the verses become, variously, chains, bars, nets, cages – instruments of capture and imprisonment.

Another feature of Hafiz's poetry was seen by the Establishment of Islam (in which, of course, there is no ordained priesthood or clergy), the supposedly learned, powerful and preachy, as sacrilege and heresy. In several verses, he disdains the commandment to go at least once in life on a pilgrimage to Mecca. He says he makes the pilgrimage to his beloved's alley, by which he means he attains closeness to God and needs no symbolic pilgrimage.

The following translation/transliteration/transformation in spirit of Hafiz's 'romantic' verse are an attempt to render its essence keeping in mind that ambivalence.

Hafiz certainly deserves to be as well known in translation as Rumi or Omar Khayyam, and one hopes that a modest offering of a selection of his Ghazals, his main oeuvre, his Rubaii, the quatrains, and his rhyming couplet offering, his limited but startling Masnavi, will establish that pre-eminence.

The first translation of Hafiz into English was undertaken by William Jones in Britain in 1772. Jones was a Persian scholar and a student of law, and was subsequently sent to India as an employee of the East India Company as a judge in Calcutta's High Court. Jones's translations of Hafiz undoubtedly stimulated the awareness of and the taste for the universe of Persian literature that awaited translation. Matthew Arnold's Rustam and Sohrab was probably the famous production of the awareness, but was soon accompanied or eclipsed by Edward Fitzgerald's immortal translation of the Rubaiyat of Omar Khayyam.

The first editions of Hafiz in Persian were published by Upjohn's Calcutta Press in 1791, giving translators of several European nationalities the volumes from which they produced English, French and German translations.

How should Persian poetry, with its forms, its metric and rhyming disciplines, its dedicated purposes and persistent conventions of metaphor and imagery, be translated into English?

The question was posed even in 1791 and justifiably persists to this day. William Jones chose to render the verse in rhyme and metre. The favoured metre of Rumi and of several of Hafiz's works was, a few hundred years before Shakespeare, the pentameric iamb. Rumi's Masnavi is written entirely in rhyming couplets as is the Masnavi of Hafiz, translated in rhyming couplets in this selection.

Professor A.J. Arberry, late of Pembroke College, Cambridge, scholar of Oriental languages and renowned translator from Persian says of Hafiz:

'... he is the writer of utmost charm and delicacy, and any version which makes him unreadable or ridiculous is obviously on wrong lines. Rhymed translation is always something of an acrobatic performance: translation in monorhyme might be likened to setting an elephant to cross a tightrope.'

This latter stricture is Arberry's judgement on nineteenth-century translators such as John Payne, who set out to reproduce in English the 'monorhyme' which many Persian poets, including Hafiz, use in their poems. The discipline is using the same word or phrase to rhyme with itself in successive lines:

An example is 'Even the Rain' by Agha Shahid Ali:

What will suffice for a true-love knot? Even the rain?
But he has bought grief's lottery, bought even the rain.

Hafiz uses monorhyme in his ghazals, but Arberry is right to parody the attempt to reproduce this in translation. In one of the translations below, we have attempted to reproduce in English this difficult form – hoping the elephant gets to the end of the tightrope.

In his introduction to Hafiz (*The Rubaiyat of Omar Khayyam and Other Persian Poems*; J.M Dent 1954) Arberry writes: 'So far no successful translation into the modern unrhymed and rhythmic cadences has been published ...'

It may be that in the sixty-six years since that was written, there are, in print, several versions of successful translations that are unrhymed and follow no poetic rhythmic pattern. The few that I have accessed are either literal and therefore appeal in ungrammatical, garbled English as gobbledygook or they are vanity projects written to give the 'translator' and the reader the conceit of immersing themselves in spirituality of some sort. Try this attempt for instance:

All the hemispheres in heaven
Are sitting around a fire
Chatting

While stitching themselves together
Into the Great Circle inside of
You.

(Tr. Daniel Ladinsky)

There can certainly be all sorts of shapes in heaven, including hemispheres, but how hemispheres, or for that matter trapezoids or cubes, sit around a fire and chat and, at the same time, take needle and thread to stitch themselves together – while chattering mind you – is not an easy image to grasp or even a pleasing one, if you manage it. And how then do they travel from heaven and their campfire to the Great Circle inside a reader? Or does the capital 'Y' of 'You' indicate a divine being in whom heaven resides?

Wouldn't the conceit of the reader – the sort who extols this manner of translation on some internet forum, believe that the circle was inside him or her?

Or consider this:

O fool, do something, so you won't just stand there
looking dumb.
If you are not traveling and on the road, how can
you call yourself a guide?

In the School of Truth, one sits at the feet of the
Master of Love.
So listen, son, so that one day you may be an old
father, too!

All this eating and sleeping has made you ignorant
and fat;
By denying yourself food and sleep, you may still
have a chance.

Know this: If God should shine His lovelight on
your heart,
I promise you'll shine brighter than a dozen suns.

And I say: wash the tarnished copper of your life
from your hands;
To be Love's alchemist, you should be working with
gold.

Don't sit there thinking; go out and immerse yourself in
God's sea.
Having only one hair wet with water will not put
knowledge in that head…

(Tr. Thomas Raine Crowe)

These fragments undoubtedly serve the purpose of enticing the reader into believing that he or she has entered some irrational dimension where you need to 'deny yourself food and sleep' because you feel ignorant and fat. Is that same internet reader and fan feeling addressed and even chastised by the admonition? But hey! It's spiritual, dude!

Immersing oneself in a sea and getting all your hair wet may be a path to enlightenment if the sea is God or at least belongs to him. But why anyone who hasn't entered the sea has only one wet hair is not clear. Some Persian tradition or assumption in Hafiz's original may have made that clear, but in Mr Crowe's verse, it sits a bit uneasily.

Whatever effect these lines, and so many like them from so many 'translators' and self-proclaimed Sufi masters, have on the reader, they aren't poetic renderings of Hafiz's poetry. Not that all poetry should make rational sense. It may evoke a response in one or other of our five senses – or it may make music in words as the work of Whitman and Eliot proves.

Edward Fitzgerald's translation of the Rubaiyat of Omar Khayyam remains the most outstanding achievement in that it conveys the essence, if not all the nuanced contentions of Sufism, but endows them with musical, sensuous and, even on occasion, sensual charm in perfect poetic form.

The translations of Hafiz, from those of William Jones through the work of Gertrude Bell, of Reynold Nicholson and of Arberry himself are verses with the disciplines and charm of rhyme and metre. 'Poetry' remains in the eye or judgement of the reader of verse. The elevation of the latter to the status of 'poetry' will always be contentious, but in every language a cannon exists which implicitly defines or gives us clues as to poetic worth.

My attempt in the following verses is to reproduce the intention of Hafiz's lines in rhyme and, as far as feasible, in the rhythm he adopted. The cadences of Persian and English being different, the rhythmic rendering was in many of the genres linguistically acrobatic or impossible. No contemporary idiom or style of verse seemed appropriate to this transliteration, though it consciously avoids, for instance, racy American-English phrases and constructions.

The verses in this random selection are divided into three sections: The Rubaiyat, or quatrains, the Ghazals, the Masnavi and some fragments from Hafiz's work which appeal as aphoristic. The Rubaii are single verses with the a,a,b,a rhyme scheme. The Ghazals are traditionally love songs of varying lengths and of several forms, but in Hafiz's hands they are in the main addressed to the ambivalent object of his longing as discussed above. His verses don't leave us with any indication whether the object of a line or address is one or the other, though scholars tell us that the later poems are clearly in the tradition of spiritual verse. The Masnavi is a form in which rhyming couplets follow a larger theme.

FIRDOUS ALI

(written in tribute to the late Firdous Ali by Farrukh Dhondy)

Firdous Ali, who died in London two years before this compilation was complete and published, was an accomplished linguist and translator. He was born in Kashmir and came to Britain in his twenties to study dentistry.

He qualified but never practised and turned his hand instead to community work, advising other Asian immigrants on their rights and procedures with government associations and other institutions.

He was proficient in Kashmiri, Urdu, Persian, Punjabi and English. He had a prodigious knowledge of the poetry of Indian and Persian languages, and an encyclopaedic knowledge of the history of Indian cinema. He could tell you every major or minor actor's list of films from the start of the film industry to the present day. He knew which songs were composed and sung by whom, and in which year. In both these respects, he was a human computer.

He was appointed by UK TV's Channel 4 to acquire and translate the Indian and Pakistani films and serials it transmitted. His catalogue of films sub-titled in precise English has been the stock of a score of TV stations since.

Firdous was what, in any culture, would be called a 'character', always eager to demonstrate his vast store of facts. At an actor's funeral in Mumbai, as the presiding priest was giving the peroration, he stood up in the audience and rudely corrected the biographical facts in the speech. He was asked to leave. He was known, as a guest at dinner parties, to remark loudly that he wouldn't feed his hostesses' s cooking to his dogs.

Apart from this eccentricity of untoward outspokenness, Firdous was one of the most generous human beings, with his time, with his money and his never-ending hospitality. This collaborator and friend misses him.

fd.

Note on the Collaboration

FIRDOUS Ali reading Hafiz in Persian to Farrukh Dhondy, verbally explained the import of each verse and then wrote down the literal meaning of the words. Dhondy rendered them into the verse forms of this compilation.

The Rubaiyat

The Quatrains Of Hafiz

My eyes are full of visions of your face
Your ways the only paths my feet can trace
You bless creation with your gift of sleep
Yet keep my mind aloof from sleep's embrace

A draught of wine will set you on the way
Don't quarrel with the devil, do not stay,
Though he will try and tempt and keep you here
My beloved, come with me – don't delay!

The heavens took you from me and the theft
Has robbed me of all signs of joy and left
My lips without a smile, my empty heart
Only He and I know how bereft

My King who are all brave, all just and wise
How can you fall for their malicious lies?
Which distance you from my true loyal self?
How shall I convince you – in which disguise?

A friend, some wine, the finest things in life
The longing that her kisses were as rife
As the wounds with which she bled my poor heart
O surgeon come again and wield your knife

I fell under the pious influence
Of friends who urged me to vow abstinence
Throughout the spring. Then asked the nightingale
'You fool, why in this season of incense?'

They are most fortunate who walk in ways
That lead to you as all their nights and days
And hearts are filled with radiance from you –
Then what of those who can't afford this praise?

Your tresses like pure rays of light cascade
Upon me. You are moonlit night and shade.
The perfume of your presence is the dusk,
Your countenance the pride of dawn's parade

The hour arrives when parting from my friends
I fall to brooding as my mood descends
Into sobriety. What good is wine
Without the joys that companionship lends?

This vision held me in paralysis
But would not lift her veil and so dismiss
The doubts I had that she was not The One
'So, if I'm not, don't ask me for a kiss!'

My heart has bled with longing for The One
Who is beyond the grasping reason's un-
Comprehending sterility. O when
Will the veil of that stranger be undone?

You are that moon that holds the sun in thrall
The contradiction of eclipse and all
The earth glitters and even heavens bow –
How can the shooting stars neglect to fall?

The bird ensnared does sing in sorrow still
The sword of loss shines, sharpened now to kill
All hope of a reprieve from this torment
This draught that doth my cup of sorrow fill

The music of your tresses lightly trips
Through my sight. Your faintly parted lips
Suggest and promise that elusive kiss
Which can release my heart from this eclipse?

No restlessness can excel that of mine
No flagon can fulfil this thirst for wine
Your tresses are my anchor and my cage
This trap of madness – ecstasy divine!

Like spring which comes to valleys and to hills
Suspend your reason, give way to the thrills
That follow the fast beating of your heart,
The promise that the spring of love fulfils

When I was out singing beneath the stars
A ray from Venus struck – or was it Mars?
It spread this longing through my blood and veins
Without you how can I endure these hours?

A bud first feels the caress of the light
To blossom as a rose and bless our sight
With colours pink and red. Just so, my love
Open yourself to me – what need for fright?

When shooting stars cross horizons by day
They burn unnoticed, streaking on their way
So, let us celebrate our secret love
With ecstasy - without vulgar display.

You know that 'love' will be today's discourse,
Tomorrow we shall speak of love, of course!
What else can occupy our hearts and minds
Whose origin is love – their only source?

Last night I caught the sickness of the stars
It came I think from Venus, not from Mars
It is contagious, passed on by a kiss
So, come and share these dark ecstatic hours

The rose feels the encouragement of light
And blossoms with its fragrance to delight
The senses. So must we open to love
And escape the all-inhibiting blight.

Her beauty and her wit are unsurpassed
O captive Heart, she's made you beat so fast
Delicate lips, the flower in her cheeks
Her form, her speech, in sweet syllables cast …

This wine, this ecstasy, come let us drink
This essence of existence, feel and think
Of spring and flowers and gatherings of friends
The joys of Life, this ephemeral blink!

Tall as a cypress the moon in the sky
Held up her mirror, I suppressed a sigh.
I pledged my honour, placed it at her feet
'Don't be absurd' was her abrupt reply.

How can I bear this burden of my heart?
This separation is a cruel dart
Piercing my existence – where is she?
Why does she choose to live a life apart?

The company of learned men may be
A bitter pill. Regard it as honey
And though the company of fools beguile
It is the poison of duplicity.

Pluck the rose of love from off the tree
The wealth of life is love. It is the key
And fountain from which Hazrat Khizar drank
The draught that bestows immortality

I know my love no differently from those
Who don't know love. The grief within me grows
As I observe the obduracy of
This world and how my insanity flows

O Hafiz, why didn't you understand
The Mystery that underlies this grand
Design, this universe you only glimpse
The painting, but never the Painter's hand

The story isn't over, but it's dawn
I give thanks for infinities unborn
And for the endless sauciness of Time
And for that brief glimpse when her veil was torn

For friendship Ḥafiz you must pay the price
Which does mean suffering and sacrifice
And tolerating all her tyrannies
Just being close to her has to suffice

Your image is the mirror of my soul.
I want that image, chaste, complete and whole
To pass into my eyes – alas the thorns
Of my eyelashes are out of control

The wine of love, its intoxication
Is poisoned with threats of dissipation –
The moistened eye, the heart consumed in fire
My loss in her, my ego's degradation

Today as a surprise there came a rose
Sent by a shy lover, I must suppose
A floral substitute expressing love
Its fragrance matching all its outward shows

Renounce the pleasures of the world my son
Search for the hidden message of The One
Who is the light on light, the life, The Face
Then all your pilgrimages you may shun

The ultimate can never be embraced
By those who pursue wealth or those who waste
Their time on earth in sensual retreats
So pray with words, like pearls, my friend – make haste!

Pour me the wine my sacred guide did bless
That I may engage with life's complex chess
And make me oblivious of living's faults
That I may know what mortals only guess

Your eloquence is yet no guarantee
That when her veil is lifted you will see
The face of The Beloved. Your desire
Must qualify, its longing is the key

To those who shun the pleasures that I crave
In the hope that their abstinence will save
Them from perdition, Hafiz says that wine
Will cause life's perfume to rise from his grave

A slave of The Beloved, at her beck
And call – I wear her collar round my neck
I am the pawn of this opposing Queen
Who on the chequered board can mate and check!

No riches compensate a life of woe
No pleasures can negate the pains that grow –
Though all the joys of seven thousand years
Are hostages to this life's fleeting show

I knew one day you'd leave, I did foretell
That moment of your parting would compel
This torment, this salt in my wounded heart
And now it's here, that ultimate farewell

Now is the time to embrace all delight
To celebrate with music, wine and sight
Of The Beloved! Life is fleeting past
They say the day is pregnant with the night

But equally the night begets the day
Something the proverbs don't bother to say
How could these produce offspring without mates?
– Or is that just mysterious nature's way?

They say there will be wine in paradise
And seventy-two virgins! Are these lies?
Why should I mend my ways to get me there,
While I partake of what this life supplies?

So, in this life I crave my heart's desire.
If unfulfilled, then let my soul retire
To that beyond where doors of heaven yield
Wine and houris in unveiled attire.

What profit is there in the gambler's throw?
What profit can this joyless world bestow
Upon me, save for the light of my eyes?
O shine on me, Beloved, do not go!

The nightingale will serenade the rose
Who strikes a budded, closed conceited pose
The nightingale persists in eloquence
Until the rose opens its lips and glows

To Sufis what does music signify?
The rhythm that makes burning passions sigh
And subside – as the nurse who holds a child
And rocks it to sleep with a lullaby

The sun in splendour, Venus like the moon
Appeared together in the dawn and soon
The day broke out and yet the sun was gone
O Hafiz that's a paradoxic tune!

My broken heart in this court stands accused –
Your witnesses and verdict are confused –
O Qazi, can't you see that they are drunk
And frivolous – so I must be excused!

My love for You has brought me lasting grief
Which turned to tears which flow without relief
I watch your beauty grow, my conscience shrinks
I know you now, my poor sanity's thief!

The world is by the lure of wealth ensnared
Like Narcissus who at his image stared
And thought his visage was the most beautiful thing
And vanity its victory declared!

The best time to drink wine is in your youth:
Intoxication blunts the sharpened tooth
Of this world's ignorant and wicked ways
So, flee through wickedness from wicked truth!

My love for the Beloved you demean
My bruised heart's hurt and pain remain unseen
O Sufi, make concessions for the weak
The excesses of this poor libertine

The ruby wine is poured into the glass
The Companion and Confidante, Alas!
Must assess all human mortality
Forget it! Let the refilled chalice pass

I grasped my Beloved's tresses and she
Said, 'Let these strands of dark idleness be
Let them go and take my lips instead
We don't want long life, we want gaiety'

I grieve because we still remain apart
Every moment is like a sharpened dart
That draws the blood from my eyes through the night
The daybreak won't relieve my forlorn heart

The valiant who uprooted Khaibar's gate
The generous gift of Quabar's Master's fate –
Ask O Hafiz who or what these were
The Saki will your thirst thus satiate

O friend shield yourself from all enmity;
Seek The One who is demure and pretty
Shun the company of the ignorant
And foolish – they don't deserve your pity

From Babil your eyes derived sorcery
The mad spell of your tresses captured me –
All Hafiz's verses are there to serve
The One who has inspired this slavery

The Queen of all the gardens is the Rose
Even the tallest, proudest cypress knows
Whose beauty summons the cloud's frequent tears
Whose fragrance around the whole planet blows

When She of the Black Mole takes off her dress
Then through her naked breast her heart's caress
Is as clear to sight as the black stone
Viewed through the crystal water's playfulness

I gave my life to The Beloved's quest
A pursuit that lends the seeker no rest
Does His indifference mean He is my foe?
Or is my pain another mortal test?

O Friend, forget desires of the past
Our lives are loaned to us and will not last
Don't look to heaven to provide the wine
Enter the tavern with your eyes downcast

I would keep faith in friendship – make it so!
No relief from this pain – but fake it so!
You are my life, my Friend to whom I owe
My love – I could never forsake it so!

Our separation causes me to weep
Just as a burning candle cannot keep
Itself from shedding tears as it dies
In restless dreams the sound of music creeps

The bird of Joy in music spreads its wings
The blossoming garden its fragrance flings
And does the breeze speak to me of her breasts?
Or am I just imagining these things?

Beloved, when I spent the night with you
And from your lips immortality drew
All human fear of death then passed away
Your nectar bestowed life on me anew

My longing for your caress and your kiss
Remain with me – a memory of bliss
My lips now utter just one sentiment
Come back! Come back! There is no phrase but this!

My love for you has left me with this grief
It's stolen all composure like a thief
Who crept into the window of my heart
And left me sorrow – sorrow without relief

The sweet and bitter mingle in each sip
You take from the eternal goblet's lip
To teach you the true purpose of this world
Not for a moment should that goblet slip

The Beloved said 'Look I am the moon'
The radiant orb, the starry sky's balloon –
But that's only today – it will be lean
And slender, like my lover's body, soon!

O Breeze, my roving friend, convey my plight
To One curled in the cradle of the night –
She sleeps oblivious of my affliction
This longing that has put all rest to flight

Who else will defend you – except myself?
Who will recommend you – except myself?
But I'll spread lies of your malevolence
So none will befriend you – except myself!

The sun and moon in dignified array
Shine down on humble dust by night and day
So do not beg me with your eye or heart
To sit in silence and neglect to pray

You traverse the wilderness of desire
Feeling you are even immune to fire
And tempted to enter the lion's mouth
– Then no more hunts – he'll swallow you entire

O Hafiz why persist in telling tales?
Your pen may follow hypocrisy's trails
Why not enter the tavern, fill the cup
And savour all that drunkenness entails?

Your almighty power created me;
Through life your love nourished me tenderly
Now sinning for at least a hundred years
I'll test your benevolence and mercy

Beloved the un-blossomed bud is shy
And drunk Narcissus wanders, wondering why –
The rose derives its radiance from the moon
And the moon reflects His light from on high

O breeze, there is a message I must send
For my love's ears alone, so kindly wend
Your way to her and tell her of my grief
In words and whispers which will not offend

Your eyes betray your cunning and conceit
They drip with drops of mad aggressive heat
Soon you'll be isolated from all friends
Your eyes then will rain tears of defeat

Beloved place the flagon on my palm –
I'm mad with passion – wine may make me calm
Or chain me with your tresses, hold me down
Before I do myself this passion's harm

Your almond eyes and pistachio-like lips
Have cast my senses into dark eclipse
So be my Saki, I can be your friend
Who behind closed doors from your chalice sips

My Beloved said patience was the test
That would put every beating heart to rest
The heart that seeks love is a drop of blood
A thousand worries crowd it in this quest

God has given us one tongue and two ears
Intending that one talks less than one hears
The ignorant should only speak up when
Questioned by wiser beings like Sufi seers

How unequal is captivity's deal!
I am helpless and so in love I feel
So meek I'd sit on fire at your beck
And you from my glances would even steal

Don't keep company with the libertine
The players in this planet's grievous scene
The Sufi who lifts up the cup of wine
Is declared by the hypocrites unclean

Union is short and separation's long
To measure them as equal is quite wrong
Alas! As written in the book of life
They are but mortal joys and sorrow's song

Youth has fled from my body and my soul
Still leaving me the mounted rider's role
With my feet in stirrups and reins in hand
Old age notwithstanding I take control!

A secluded corner, kebabs and wine
The music of a harp and flute divine
And She, what could I ask for heaven more
I'd Hakim Tai's generosity decline

Lion of God, Ali, destroy the claws
Of those who ravage truth and defy laws
O Divider of Heaven and of Hell
Have mercy on this creation of yours

The Beloved sat on his royal throne
And asked if I would worship Him alone
'You are no child and full of sin,' he said
'And at your age for that you must atone'

APHORISTIC VERSES

If humans realized what wine was worth
They would not sleep till they had filled the earth
With vines watered by streams scented with rose
Protected by four walls and within those
Some pretty Turkish maidens wearing capes
To fan the flies off the ripening grapes

Give me but a glimpse of your divine face
And I shall be a wisp of foliage blown
Away by the windy storm and leave no trace
Or like the flood uproot the founding stone

The world is but a passing show, my friend
A final curtain will proclaim the end
For all the travellers on this trodden stage
Whom time assigns some lines, then tears the page
So learn your lines and speak them without fear
The last line reads 'There is no stopping here!'

Worrying never earned a sou
So please find something else to do

One night, Hafiz, the moon to me confessed
That her celestial life with love was blessed
The Sun, her lover lent her light to shine
As the full moon and gradually to decline

And become a bright crescent in the sky
And then I heard this maiden crescent cry
'O Hafiz is my destiny to turn
Into a flaming orb and must I burn

Into the blush of love?' So I replied
'Come my friend and sit here by my side;
You are the moon that waxes and then wanes
So, each of us must be what He ordains'

Mountaineers say they climb because it's there
Come climb the heights of love and hold my hand
Firmly and don't let go because this land
Is full of hazard, pitfall, trap and snare

My heart like a bird was caught in a snare
The dagger of grieving placed on its neck
It longed for the freedom to float in the air
But was trapped in this body, its ruin and wreck

Love is the song of the sweet bird of youth
So why do we crave immortality?
If it's without love, I tell you the truth,
I pray every day that it would rather not be!

My house was full of confusion and pain
My heart was racked with doubt and cold despair
Until my Friend came visiting again
And expelled every fear which lingered there

If they emanate from the wise
Poisoned words are honeyed and sweet
In the company of fools
Even proverbs of heaven retreat

I wander in your street, a vagabond,
And though I'm here, you're still so far away
The perfume of your tresses is a wand
That conjures up the madness I display

GHAZALIYAT

1

See the rose that has blossomed red in bloom
And hear the springtime Bulbul's joyous song
The tavern's doors are open and the throng
Is raising glasses in the crowded room

Hafiz, before you thought to venture here
With repentance as heavy as a rock
That weighed you down, you thought that wine would mock
All your regrets and bring you drunken cheer

So fill the cup and drink the strong red wine
The slaves and sultans like you crave a drink
As, before wine, the world's distinctions shrink
We stand before Him stripped, an equal line

And when the feast of life on earth is done
The revellers all step into the night
Into the dark or into radiant light?
They cannot know – and yet they go as one!

So Hafiz continue to sing and praise
All Life and thank the Divine Love supreme
And let your verses all reflect the theme
That runs through time and all our human days.

2

I swore myself to temperance in the spring
And smugly thought I did a righteous thing
But soon realized that temperance was the wine
That made the stars and constellations sing

My love came last night to me in my dreams
And assailed me with beauty as the sun
Will cause the naked eye to look away
And yet I gazed upon the sublime one

My dreaming sight bypassed the use of eyes
Don't question 'how?' – believe that it was done

A drunken Narcissus who sees his face
Reflected in the stream but cannot trace
The identity of the features there
Rippled by the wine's heady embrace
Is not as half besotted as I am
By the Beloved's allure and her grace

This elegance of expression has caused
The pearl, Hafiz, to hide inside its shell
And even daylight crawls inside her veil
Each dusk because, Hafiz, you rhyme so well!

3

My eyes are filled with tears, I cannot see
Though wine dispels all fears, I cannot see
I know the light God gives man is love
Yet all is darkness and I cannot see

No drinker ever offers me a cup,
There is no font of generosity,
They say the sun's the closest burning star
Another quite so bright I cannot see

Lost in my lover's dark cascading locks
I'm blind to all visual reality
And there bewildered eyes are bound to stay
No mirror can reveal her face to me

So now my only solace is in wine
To drown in that intoxicating sea
And compose verses defying life's flow
Inventing showers of pearls I did not see.

4

The sky is a blue ocean spread above
With stars that swim like fishes in the sea
And planets like the mighty whales immersed

For us these are all heavenly signs of love
O Hafiz rejoice in this ecstasy
Rejoice in His game till your heart shall burst …

4A

(An alternative translation)

The sky is blue like some suspended sea
The stars are like bright fishes swimming free
The planets are the whales I ride upon
The sun and all its light have fused in me

So in this cosmic frame what are the rules
That govern this wild playground? Oh, you fools
The lesson of this symphony of light
Is universes die when passion cools.

5

A fellow once approached me with a boast
That he was seeing visions of The Friend
He wouldn't stop – it was enough to send
Me round the bend. His conceit was the most

Absorbed and self-deluding trash. I said
'Brother tell me how many goats you own!'
He looked at me as though I had just grown
Two heads. The question went down like a lead

Balloon. 'I tell you of my divine dreams
And you interrupt me with this absurd
Enquiry about goats within my herd?'
I said 'My question isn't what it seems

So brother please just count them in your mind.'
Though he was puzzled he said 'Sixty-two!'
And I said 'Great! Now brother tell me true
How many wives you have? I hope you're kind

To them. The truth is I don't want to know
The precise number but how many rose
Bushes do you cultivate, what else grows
In your orchards? And in the winter snow

Do you go out and feed the birds with grain?'
He thought it strange but answered best he could.
'You asked me if your visions were all good
Omens. So now allow me to explain

That visions, omens and the like are true
Only if they can make you feel as one
With all creation. Ask what you have done
To know whether The Friend is within you.

6

'If God would reach down from heaven and kiss
You, Hafiz, how on earth would you respond?'
'What a question! I'd feel quite drunk and this
Would set my mind and mouth muttering rogue
Verses in my inebriated bliss.'

7

I begin to skip like a child
For no reason
I float like a leaf up to the sun
In the windy season

Holding a conference, singing wild songs
A flock of birds settles on my head
Sharing between them wine and bread

So I begin to laugh and love
For every conceivable reason

Fluttering as that dancing leaf
I seek the cheek of Him I must kiss
And dissolve in myself – a selfless bliss!

8

True compassion means never thinking ill
Of others; but my brothers, it's a skill
That very few of us truly possess
And if the truth is told I must confess

The only way to learn this skill is through
Befriending Him, and from that friendship you
May learn compassion, this true elegance
To watch but never judge the human dance.

9

When you plant a seed your own heart grows
When you make love you speak to God who knows
You as a soul he would invite to be
At his feast which lasts through eternity
And when you sing you feed our starving world
Your laughter is the flag of sound unfurled.

10

Come close to me tonight, O passing dream
And celebrate our closeness, let it seem
A mad affair which keeps neighbours awake
When we make love all night without a break

I feel I'm giving birth to several suns
I'm holding trees and forests upside down
To gently shake the nimble deer who runs
Through thickets, on to my flowing night gown

I know you think this is all in my mind
But tricks of mind never exist for me
All dreams are real: Hafiz, you can find
One in your coat pocket, it's there to see

But let's not talk about what I can do
Tonight our talk must be all about You.

11

How many ways are there to make love?
How many curves make the branches of trees?
How many shapes does the eye discern?
And does the mind make sense of these?

The spring brings to earth an orchestra of scents
And a muddle of light on fire like my lips
And the whirl of the spheres, celestial events
Dimensions unknown, the meteor which slips

In a fiery arch beyond the earth's air
Proclaiming that He is everywhere.

12

The mean are dedicated to confine
All humans in logic and reason's cage;
But while the moon is low at night the sage
Emerges with his draft of love divine

To distribute to all the cage's key
And set the joyful, rowdy prisoners free.

13

Come let us scatter roses, pour the wine
Reach up and pull and tilt the sky's incline

If grief become a monster and attack
The cup-bearer has means to fight him back

O Singer, with your harp and dulcet voice
Play on my heart-strings, sing and I'll rejoice

O Morning Breeze, this body is but dust
To be blown to where she keeps beauty's trust

All boasts of love and miracles are lies
So stop your prattle and apologize

And come with me to where the Saki plies
Us with the very fount of paradise

Pour essence of the rose into your wine
And burn the aloe for fragrance divine

O Lover, let your presence bring the light
That inspires the odes that we recite

As Shiraz shuns all poet's eloquence
Come, Hafiz, and depart from hither hence.

14

God is my witness, I did caution all
Those I destroyed through love's fatal pitfall

O Saki, you know that your eyes are cups
That hold the wine on which my poor heart sups

Two strangers meet and make love through the night
I was sceptical, but now I am contrite

He comes as Love, bereft of gifts to give
I'll welcome Him as long as I shall live

The loss of love has caused me so much grief
My sea of tears has been my sole relief

Beware the pain of burning, shun the fire
Beware the flames of longing and desire

She was called Shararat, she was the one
Who set fire to the Judgement Day's Sun.

15

If she wounds my heart I will not cry
Love's arrow is a welcome shaft to bear
Her bow-like brows and missiles of her stare
Have conquered me, I am willing to die

The sorrows of the world weigh down my heart
My only consolation fills the cup
Unbearable the night when we're apart
O Sun, come swallow melancholy up

O mullah mine, you promise paradise
With honeyed milk and heavy-laden trees –
I am the bird whose twitter on the breeze
Calls out to Gabriel's abode in the skies

I beg you, dear Saki, tell the truth
Will this sweet draught of wine restore my youth?

16

The body is the earthly veil of soul
And when the veil is torn and so reveals
The wonder of the spirit and the whole
Face of self, which like a caged bird
Longed to sing of that same paradise
From whence we came, O let the song be heard
For it is all – we know not why we are
Confined to earth and gravity's embrace
The soul should soar in heaven like a star

Though it be trapped within the body's space

The scent of love accumulates like musk
In my heart's blood and from there emanates
From out my body, from this earth-bound husk
For the release my soul anticipates

If paradise is where the soul belongs
Why do my feet to humble taverns lead
O do not judge me, all my rights and wrongs
Are symptoms of the ceaseless pain that feeds
On separation from celestial mist
O Hafiz, how you long not to exist!

17

Alexander's magic glass revealed
The state of every place he'd overrun
From other mortals these truths were concealed
No pose or posture imitates The One

Who is the fount of love, it's devotee –
The Sufi caught up in the cosmic dance
Did not attain that state, he is not free
Through adopting some costume or a stance

The world is like an ocean in my eyes
And in that ocean I have learned to drown
Into the peace of love, where logic dies
And gold emerges from the muddy brown

The pupil of my eye reflects the mole
On my beloved's cheek, I know its worth
To me is sight itself. I see this whole
Countenance, the Sun, the Stars, the Earth

I lost my mad enamoured heart in yours –
What else can a weak Son of Adam do?
These tyrannies are in our instincts burned
From birth – but Love and Kindness must be learned

So do not pray to ask for things, for greed
That's arrogant for He knows what you need!

18

You gave me sight to see my love and yet
How can I repay such a heavy debt

O tell the lover not to wash his face
The dust of life all lovers must embrace

Oh Khwaja, you have shed your share of tears
And marvelled at success when it appears

Prepare yourself for prayer with all your heart
True prayer is that which takes your soul apart

Do not deviate from the mystic path
Let it lead you to this life's aftermath

Though there be trials all along the way
The goal is heaven, traveller do not stray

The cup is but a metaphor for grace
Ignore the distractions of this sad place

Why should I heed the whispers of the breeze
When the tall cypress whispers lies like these?

Your beauty is indifferent to my sighs
Persistence is my fate, I realize

Venus's song echoes – a tempting choice
Until Hafiz's verse raises its voice!

19

O Saki, float me on the sea of wine!
You nullify a kindness with a boast!
Show me the tavern door, I'll raise a toast
Saki, please point the way, give me a sign!

Then fill the cup with colours of the rose
Though the Rose still harbours in its heart
A spark of envy. I'll drink and depart
Inebriate – Oh how Her laughter flows!

If you want the sun aglow at night
Unveil the bounteous daughter of the grape
And let my eyes feast on that beauteous shape
Which brings into the darkness primal light!

And when I die don't bury me in dust
Pickle me instead in a cask of wine
In there my soul unites with the divine –
O Hafiz, hush! – They will do what they must!

My friend, when you can bear life no more
And fortune and all favours tend to stray
Then shoot a star and watch it fly away
And pierce Fortune's rotten apple core

If Hafiz wanders a hair's breadth from You
Your remedy is not far from your hand:
Just grasp your tresses, separate a strand
And trap him as the cobra-catchers do.

20

My earthly body is a veil of soul
O remove it and so reveal the whole

The sweet-voiced bird should not be in this cage
O set it free, its freedom will assuage

The thirst that constantly asks how and why
We are sent to earth's prison to live and die

My body holds me, how can I embrace
The cosmic soul, when will I see his face?

Celestial virgins are promised to those
Who will obey the book – O Hafiz, close

The door of the wine-cellar once you're in –
You're doomed to follow this salvation's sin

So outwardly my appearance is smart
Though inwardly it hides my broken heart

Come take away Hafiz's life because
The existence in which I melt is yours!

21

Your shadow over me will now suffice
To bring me riches – incense, myrrh and spice

For many years fortune forsook my door
Your shadow on it brings me joy and more

When you grace all my dreams, for heaven's sake
Why would I ever wish to stay awake?

An empty sky – a songbird did appear
My life is full of music when you're here

You are my perfumed candle in the dark
You are its soul and its igniting spark

No physician understands my disease
Or that Your absence breeds these miseries

I found your house, you said 'go fetch your stuff!'
I said 'I'll stay – these nothings are enough!'

The Pleiades were poetry for a king
My verse for You is no inferior thing

From kings to slaves all humans take their ranks
I am Her slave for which I must give thanks.

22

I was the candle closeted till dawn
When You lit up the world – You are the morn –

Your beauty marks my consciousness, no doubt
That from my grave fresh violets will sprout

I am alone, abandoned and bereft
And yet somehow, I know You have not left

My eyes are mirrors, your reflection glows
A brightness which is mine – no one else knows

The buds will blossom and the blooms will wave
When You pass as a breeze over my grave.

23

I boasted that I was the humblest man
Who crossed, these forty years, the tavern door
The tavern-keeper's blessing overran
My fate and cup – O, who could ask for more?

So do not judge me though I crave the dregs
My ragged gown is soiled but I am chaste
The falcon on the Royal glove now begs
To return to the nest he left in haste

The nightingale is trapped within a cage
Its spirit silenced by captivity
Is this my Persia? Hafiz, vent your rage
Upon its meanness and iniquity

And fill your broken body with earth's wine
Your judgement comes when you face the divine.

24

True love was never won by outward show
Mirrors can't reflect what the heart should know

No tilted cap and no conceited pose
Are substitutes for what Sikander knows

A strand of feeling thinner than a hair
Can insulate a love against despair

O save me from the ocean of my sight
Your storminess is, to my eyes, delight!

Bring on your charms, their alchemy unfold
And turn my leaden vision into gold!

25

O Sufi, you are not a creature pure –
Your foibles and temptations must endure
The tests of human nature and desire
Your tattered soul consigned to *jhannath's* fire

O Sufi, answering the muezzin's cry
Each morning to your prayers. The day goes by
But as the sun sets out the tavern door
You stagger sodden, mystic to the core

If the touchstone of truth is experience
The liars would stand naked, driven hence
When word and fact in truth have to collide
The fools and frauds have nowhere they can hide

The slaves to earthly pleasure will not reach
Salvation. Libertines should master each

Luxurious pleasure; Sufis take control
By losing it in pleasures of the soul!

The image of the Saki in my wine
Reflections of the countenance divine
Is as a warning filling me with fears
Of indulgence punished in bloody tears

Intelligence should dispel all sorrow
And seek in wine some solace to borrow
While we abide and suffer in this world
And then into eternity are hurled

O Hafiz, trade your prayer-carpet and quilt
For wine – and do it with no tinge of guilt
If but the moon-faced Saki serves the wine
What need of prayer, you've merged with the divine.

26

Not everyone who worships
Is confident of His embrace
O mirror-gazer, don't think
That you gaze upon Sikander's face

When you pretend to his wisdom
Without having run his race

Don't imagine that tilting your cap
Or adopting an arrogant stare
Can counterfeit the stance
Or lend you a Majestic air

These don't even suggest
The burdens sovereignty has to bear

The paths of love are as narrow
As this my beloved's hair
And each separate moment is a dot
In the progress of Time's despair

Not every bald head at a shrine
Is some Qalandar beyond compare

My sight becomes an ocean
Of everything I see
I feel that I am drowning
In the world's reality

And sorry for those who cannot swim
In the waves and this tide with me

The round pupil of my eye
Is as black as the rounded mole
Upon The Beloved's holy cheek
The dot that defines my sole

And unique pearl. O jeweller,
You must now its worth extol!

27

On seeing The Beloved
My poor enamoured heart
Was lost in riotous ecstasy
And all reason did depart

This poor progeny of Adam
Became an ethereal upstart!

The spoils of tyranny
And brutality are cheap
To earn the way of justice
You undertake the steep

Climb up to realms of right
And the world is then yours to keep

Do not beg God for baubles
Or become a slave of need
Attachment to the world of want
Is tantamount to greed

The Lord is munificent
He will all the hungry feed!

To understand the verses
Or apprehend the drift
Of the lines that Hafiz did
From the maze of language sift

You must wrap yourself in innocence
And in Persian's rhapsodic gift.

28

The zephyr blew a gust
And diffused musk whirled
Rejuvenating the old
Making fragrant a new world

The Argawan now will flower
And bear fruit crimson and red
The narcissus blossoms with its keen eye
Enchanted to look upon each Tulip's head

The rose, a metaphor for life,
Beautifies the earth
This garden of sorrow and joy
With death predicted at birth

The nightingale's dirge complains
Mourning the summer's end
Knowing autumn brings falling leaves
And winter will soon descend

O heart, enjoy your todays
Don't wait until your tomorrows
Seize on every moment's delights
The next one may bring sorrows

When Shaban comes just drink your fill
Pure Ramadan follows with its fasts
Don't remain thirsty till its Eid
That is, if through these months life lasts

O Singer in this gathering
Of love, sing me a fond ghazal
Abandon lyrics which predict
The obvious, they are boring, dull

I go from the mosque to the tavern
With no guilt of doing any wrong
The sermon as a pack of homilies
Lord, I would rather your fading song.

O Hafiz, you live by the grace
Of The Beloved, whereupon
The world starts to bid you farewell
For Hafiz too must pass on.

29

No Sufi's thoughts and acts
Are entirely pure
Some will send him to hell
There tortures to endure

Every morning the Sufi
Is intoxicated through prayer
By evening in the tavern
He's trapped in the Saki's snare

If all our experience
Were touchstones of the truth
They would expose the liars
And the insincere uncouth

All slaves to luxury
Can never attain the goal
Of union with The Beloved
As will every diligent soul

If the Saki's face is etched
In intoxication's flood
Then many in the tavern
Will shed tears of blood

Oh suffer not the world
Its trials and its strife
The intelligent resort
To the bubbly wine of life

Hafiz's tattered quilt
And prayer-mat are no use
Where the Saki does dispense
Intoxication's juice …

30

They preach the laws from pulpits
And extol the Prophet's ways
Only The Friend sees what they do
Away from the public gaze

The mullahs tell us to repent
Persuading all to penitence
Hypocrites were not heaven sent
Why listen to them – it makes no sense!

The infidel doesn't fear
The coming of the Judgement Day
He denies all faith in Justice
And for that his soul must pay

Allah! Bring judgement down
On the rich who defy your rules
And arrogantly sport their slaves
– Compel them to ride mules!

I'm a slave of the tavern-keeper
Who convinces me all prayer
Should only beg for beggary
And unity with The Beloved there

O beggar at the Sufi shrine!
O beggar by poverty cursed!
Seek out the Fire-temple
Where devotion relieves all thirst

Does her infinite beauty annihilate
Her infinite suitors one by one?
Disdainful of their ultimate fate
They are compelled moths unto her sun

What worth is a blind jeweller
Or a Sufi who cannot tell
The truth from lies or right from wrong
Or a precious pearl from a shell?

O Angel! With your rosary
Come pray at the tavern door
Where the progeny of Adam
Live in a trance evermore

When in the morning I wake
And from heaven hear converse
I know the celestial residents
Are memorizing Hafiz's verse.

31

Who shares the whispers of the heart
Converses with The Friend apart

O heart cast every veil aside
What need you the vain veil of pride?

Some Sufis pawned their coats for wine
The inn-keeper kept hold of mine

The mendicant's stories fade away
Hafiz's verse is alive today

I pawned my ragged cloak for wine
Exposed the sacred thread I wore
For all the world to see and say
His faith's no secret anymore

Echoes of whispered love I hear
Are the most precious to my ear

Every sip from the crystal cup
Cries to the Saki 'fill it up, fill it up!'

There's nothing else to life's endeavour
But devotion to The Friend forever

Narcissus's self-regarding will
Turned on itself and made him ill

Chinese art reflects His grace
Proudly displayed in every space

Hafiz's heart was trapped in Her tresses
To be released? – he invites your guesses!

32

O living, O life, O times of stress
I shall move to the tavern
With all that I possess

With Her, a flask, a book of verse
I'll live and thus avoid
Treacherous friendship's curse!

Hypocrite Hafiz, you are to blame –
Your lying boasts of being pious
Ought to put you to shame!

I long to be like the Cypress tree
So secluded and tall
And free of hypocrisy

Love is the burden in my breast
It invaded my bosom
Choosing it as its nest

Your tresses awaken fervent desire
The sweet breath of musk
Emanates from my soul on fire

Though burdened with love my heart is proud
A drop more will turn its image
In my heart's mirror to cloud

Do I call myself 'Hafiz': Reciter
Of the entire Quran?
– The pretence of a mere writer!

33

When with a sword She strikes, I'll stay subdued
Her piercing arrow earns my gratitude

Her glances are arrows, her eyebrows bows
Her arms will subdue me, I know She knows!

I've suffered this life's sorrows without end
A flask of wine is now my only friend

O Morning Sun of Union give me hope
As in this night of separateness I grope

O Mullah, I'm no child whom you entice
With fruit and milk that's promised in Paradise

I am the bird whose cry to heaven flows
To Sidah beyond which no angel goes

O Saki, at this age I face the truth
Offer me a draught to restore my youth?

Now swearing by Your tresses, I'll repeat
The vow to bow my head at Your bare feet

This gown of piety can never burn
A phoenix from the fire it will return!

34

Your eyelashes are arrows piercing
With temptation the tenets of belief
In innocence – and yet your eyes are sad –
Come to me so I can relieve your grief

Companion of my heart, let me remind
You that you have forgotten all your friends
But never shall the sun rise on this earth
When I forget You – that day the world ends!

Separation from You is agony
This garden's heat makes roses perspire
O Morning Wind, come cool me with your gusts
And with your healing breath put out this fire

On the night of The Journey I may reach
The realm of doe-eyed virgins in the bright
Firmament – but that's only if You will
Show me the path to heaven with Your light

The nightingale greeted me as I woke
Singing her morning's melodious refrain
I bid the Saki bring me some more wine
To sooth the hangover and last night's pain

If The Beloved choose another one
She has the right – I've none to jealousy –
But apart from Her, I can choose no love
Not even my own soul to comfort me

The Ruler of both worlds is only Love
This life is ours so that we realize
The Beloved and Saki are but one
And we earthlings are only heaven's spies

The preacher knows no secrets of this love
Or inebriation – ignore his pleas
Come with me, together we'll greet the night
With wine under the moon and Pleiades!
The message of this letter full of love
Is word-perfect, no syllable is wrong
The letter speaks of The Beloved's love
Because Hafiz dictated this whole song

35

I was granted a glimpse of Him
Accomplisher of deeds – and kind
To all his slaves. Alas! My thanks
Are to these humble words confined

You wander in the lands of need
And gather the lane's dust
Upon your face – don't wash it off
It's the elixir of lust

Lover, your heart's blood purifies
Your face and makes it fit for prayer
'If not, your prayers are vanity'
The Jurists of true love declare

O Heart! You must not deviate
From mystic paths you vowed to keep
Accept all their vicissitudes
However hard, however steep!

This world is one of sport and toys
In this life sip the cup of love
We are but travellers in this sphere
Journeying to the one above

What must I glean from the passing breeze
Which carries tales, but won't confide
Even in the upright cypress
What are these whispers breezes hide?

The Beloved's beauty is indifferent
To this stranger's love and need
And yet we strangers persevere
Though The Beloved pays no heed

Venus the songster of the skies
Has melodies with angel's wings
She cannot compete in the space
Where Hafiz with his ghazals sings.

36

O beautiful Cypress of coquetry,
This lover's hundred prayers in poetry

Are praise for the dignity of your dress
From the start of time fashioned to impress

And those who seek the scent of your desire
Must burn themselves like aloe in the fire

The enemies of truth will vainly strut
Gold doesn't lose its value when it's cut

The hapless moth burns, diving into flame
If my heart melts – your cheeks are not to blame

My heart makes pilgrimages to your lane
Then any Haj to Mecca becomes vain

No ablution or ritual compares
Your eyebrow's beauty sanctions all my prayers

O Sufi, to abstain from wine you swore
But hastened through the tavern's open door

The secret whispered by the goblets rim
Brought Hafiz, clapping, to the wine cask's brim.

37

As humble as the pilgrims to Hijaz
We lovers travel to the tavern's bars

Don't ask me, friend, for I'll only complain
Just let my tears speak to you of my pain

God made the universe to prove his art
Ayaz's beauty subdued a King's heart

My Ka'ba is now the beloved's door
I have no need of idols anymore

My separation from you made me hide
My face till I can't with my Love abide

Through long, dark nights I yearn to be with you
This blindness longs to learn to see with you

The bud conceals its secret just to tease
The zephyr blows my secret on the breeze

O Hafiz, longing for the company
Of the moon it's out of reach – can't you see

Though burning candles suffer agony
Burning may take you where you want to be.

38

O Saki, pour the wine, my generous host
Those who have done good deeds shouldn't boast

I lost my way and missed the tavern's lane
O Friend, put me on the right path again

Fill my cup with your rose-wine to the brink
That even the Rose may envy what I drink

I know I'm bad and drunk but please ignore
These outward symptoms of a shattered core

The Sun will light the deep midnight landscape
When You unveil the daughter of the grape

Don't mingle me with dust when I am dead
Bury me in a cask of wine instead

Lay the demon of all misfortune low
Shoot him with starry meteors from your bow

If Hafiz's heart by an inch transgresses
Imprison it – tie it down with your tresses.

THE MASNAVI

O wild deer, unique, gentle and kind
I keep your image always in my mind

Both poet and deer are creatures destitute
Both trepid in life's treacherous pursuit

Oh, sit with me and converse for a while
Tell me what makes you sad or makes you smile?

Tales of separation will make us sad
Let's talk of the togetherness we've had

In Love's tangled jungles of doubt and fear
No green and pleasant grazing grounds appear

O Friend, please say if you'll help those in need
Or if not you, who will the hungry feed?

Perhaps Khizar will all his blessings bring
Crowning this journey with a heart's rending?

The Quran says 'O God, don't leave me alone'
The time is nigh for sinners to atone.

The companion to a mystic Sufi
Said 'Master, one thing really puzzles me

What do you keep in your sack, is it wheat?
Or a snare to trap creatures by their feet?'

The Sufi said 'Both ample grain and tricks
I've stored to catch the Simurgh, the Phoenix!'

'How will you find the Simurgh, no one knows
If to this world the Simurgh comes or goes?'

The Sufi replied 'Everyone has heard
The legend of this great mythical bird

And I keep faith that myths are somewhere true
And in that faith this miracle pursue.

I devote my life to this mystery
Surrendering to wine which is the key

To quell the pain that Separation brings
And saturate my heart with mystic springs

A pilgrim on the path to realize
Even a glimpse of The Beloved's eyes!

O Traveller and Friend, sit by my bed
If leaving this poor world my soul has fled

O stranger, our encounter is so dear
You will stay in my heart, a souvenir

O God, who know this broken heart's desire
Whose just benevolence fills the entire

Universe, extracting each day out of night –
Just so, grant solace to relieve my plight

Our Separation brings unceasing pain
Forgive me if I constantly complain.

O Companions, our lives should have one goal
To seek with Him confluence of the soul

On joining this Caravan I was told
That patience is the virtue I must hold

Onto and never leave the Saki's room
Or the grove or garden where roses bloom

Standing in spring by the banks of the stream
Converse with yourself, let your eyes teem

With tears in memory of friends who've gone
Into the beyond. Still you look upon

The morning cloud which mimics with its rain
Your weeping eyes – though clouds can feel no pain

The Old Companion shows us no regard
O Muslim, don't conclude his heart is hard

And though He wields His unforgiving sword
Beg for His mercy, He may yet reward

You while remaining remote as The Other
When has brother done this to a brother?

Perhaps Khizar's blessings may yet unite
This wretched being with the Ultimate Light

Why should the Sun stoop to look on my need?
Why should heaven's light pay it any heed?

So clutch the pearl and shun the fingered coin
Pursuit of fame will all your life purloin!

My pen and verse explore the mysteries
O Hafiz, all your worth depends on these!

I kneaded wisdom into my soul's dough
Out of that dough the seeds of wisdom grow

Take in the fragrance of the scent of hope
Sweeter than the musk of the antelope

Your destiny is written, it's too late
To quarrel with or rearrange your fate!

From fields of love come melodies of the lute
One grain of its barley is my life's pursuit

In this place Gabriel's wings were set on fire
Children fanned the flames rejoicing at his pyre

In this place which audacious one shall speak
God is remote, through prayer do you Him seek?

O Hafiz with respect and caution sing
And be concise, he's not all-forgiving!

About the Author

Farrukh Dhondy is a British-Indian writer born in 1944 in Pune, India. He went to school and college in India and then obtained degrees from Cambridge and Leicester universities. His work includes fiction, non-fiction, journalism, stage drama, TV and films. His latest books are a life-memoir entitled *Fragments Against my Ruin* and *Hawk and Hyena,* an account of his dealings with the serial killer Charles Sobhraj.